Women of Blessing: 31 Days of Flowing in the Favor of God

Women of Blessing:
31 Days of Flowing in the Favor of God

Leann Guzman

2014

Women of Blessing:

31 Days of Flowing in the Favor of God

Copyright © 2014 by Leann Guzman

All rights reserved. This book or any portion thereof may not be reproduced or used in any manner whatsoever without the express written permission of the publisher except for the use of brief quotations in a book review or scholarly journal.

Credits
Executive Developer and Cover Art: Anthony R. Morehead
Editor: Candie McClain
Author Photo: MelissaE Smith Photography

Scriptures taken from the Holy Bible, New International Version®, NIV®. Copyright © 1973, 1978, 1984, 2011 by Biblica, Inc.™ Used by permission of Zondervan. All rights reserved worldwide. www.zondervan.com The "NIV" and "New International Version" are trademarks registered in the United States Patent and Trademark Office by Biblica, Inc.™

First Printing: 2014

ISBN 978-1-312-38943-4

www.womenofblessing.com

INTRODUCTION
The Blessing of Flowing

"And God is able to bless you abundantly, so that in all things at all times, having all that you need, you will abound in every good work." 2 Corinthians 9:8 NIV

The name of this devotion is intentional – it is not called "Blessed Women," because that would mean that we are only looking for blessing for ourselves. Instead, it is called "Women of Blessing" because not only do we want to receive blessings in our own lives, but the Lord always blesses us so we can be a blessing to others. He doesn't send us a blessing and expect it to stop. It should flow from the Lord TO you, and then AWAY from you to other people.

Blessings are always meant to flow. If you stop the flow of the blessings by only accepting and never giving, you will stagnate and will not grow in Him. Conversely, if you are always giving and never receiving from the Lord, you will run out of the ability to give because there will be nothing left.

In this devotional, we will read about numerous blessings God wants to, and promised to, give us. On each day, think specifically about how that blessing not only blesses you, but how you could let that blessing flow to those around you. Try it for the next thirty-one days, and see how life changes, and how much better it is living as His conduit of favor to those around you!

Lord, I want to be a woman of blessing. Not just a "blessed woman", but a woman to whom Your favor comes, and from whom Your favor flows. With each blessing I receive, help me find ways to pass it on to others. Thank You for the opportunity to be a conduit in the flow of Your blessings! In Jesus' name, amen.

DAY ONE
The Blessing of My Heart's Desire

"For I know the plans I have for you," declares the LORD, *"plans to prosper you and not to harm you, plans to give you hope and a future."* Jeremiah 29:11

"Take delight in the LORD and he will give you the desires of your heart." Psalms 37:4

If you're like most women, you have a few desires of the heart, a few dreams you wish would come true. Maybe a clone to help you get everything done? An all expense paid vacation? A self-cleaning house? All of the above?

You probably have some serious desires, too. But Psalms 37:4 says that our desires are met when we first delight in the Lord. The thing is that when you love the Lord so much that He actually *delights* you, it changes the desires of your heart. You start to want your will to align with His perfect will. You begin to want what He wants for your life. You start to submit to what HIS plans are for your future, and not worrying so much because you find yourself trusting Him more.

So, while our imaginations can come up with all kinds of things we might want the Lord to give us, the key to real blessings is to grow closer to Him so it is His plans and His purpose that are fulfilled in and through us on His timetable. That's when the desires of our heart are met, and the full measure of His favor and blessings is ours to enjoy.

Lord, help me to learn to delight in You, both in who You are and what You do for me. As I grow closer to You, change my heart so that my desires are in line with Your plan for me, and I can experience all of Your blessings. In Jesus' name, amen!

NOTES

DAY TWO
The Blessing of Perfection

"Therefore there is now no condemnation for those who are in Christ Jesus...." Romans 8:1

Someone once said that the space between where you are and where you think you should be is the place where the enemy wreaks havoc on you by getting you to feel hopeless, condemned, not good enough, and unworthy. He succeeds when you succumb to these feelings and don't fulfill your potential in Christ.

God's blessings for you today have nothing to do with your yesterday. When you repented and believed in Jesus, He forgot your sins. When He looks at you, He sees the perfection of Jesus, so do not let feelings of guilt or condemnation or inadequacy keep you from the fullness of God's blessings.

The Lord wants to move you out of where you've been, not so He can love you more or approve of you more, because that's not possible given His already-infinite love for you. He does, though, want to position you for maximum blessings. It is a call to come up higher without looking down, to wade in deeper without looking back. He calls to you in love.

Lord, thank You for sending Your Son for me so His blood can cover all my imperfections and I can take on His perfection as my own. Thank You for wanting to move me to where You can bless me to the maximum, and where You can use me to bless others the most. Anytime I feel guilt or inadequacy in my spiritual walk, remind me of Romans 8:1, of Your unfathomable love towards me, and of the freedom from the bondage of these feelings that Jesus purchased for me with His death and resurrection. In Jesus' name, amen!

NOTES

DAY THREE
Blessings from Jesus

"...[I]n him all things hold together." Colossians 1:17b

Jesus came to give us so much. The Bible gives us a long list of things He gives us when we are in Him or when we act through Him.

First, He gives us a completely **different relationship with God** by giving us peace with God (Romans 5:1) and confidence toward Him (2 Corinthians 3:4).

Second, He gives us a completely **different standing with the enemy** by giving us freedom from accusation (Romans 8:33), deliverance (Romans 7:25), and victory (1 Corinthians 15:57).

Third, He gives us a completely **different life**. Through Jesus, we are a new creation (2 Corinthians 5:17), and we are made complete (Colossians 1:17). He also gives us clean consciences (Hebrews 9:14) and blessings in the heavenly realms (Ephesians 1:3).

When we accept all that He is and wants to be to us, we flow in faith and blessings like never before. When we really grasp what it means to be in Christ and what it is we have through Him and what is already ours in Him, then we will enjoy those blessings for ourselves, and we will impact those around us like never before.

Lord, You have done so much for me and You really are my everything. Help me believe it and live like it, so that the blessings from You will flow through me to others. In Jesus' name, amen.

NOTES

Romans 5:1 (Peace & joy) Therefore, since we have been justified through faith, we have peace w/ God through our Lord Jesus Christ,

DAY FOUR
The Blessing of Belief

Immediately the boy's father exclaimed, "I do believe; help me overcome my unbelief!" Mark 9:24

C.S. Lewis said, "We are what we believe we are." Yesterday, we read what the Bible says about who we are in Christ. But if you don't believe it, is that what you actually are?

Let's look at it this way: If someone were to tell you that you won a million dollars and you really had but you didn't believe it, didn't do anything to claim it, and didn't live like you had it, then did you really win anything? It's yours, but you don't receive any benefit from it.

Sometimes it's hard to believe the good news of what the gospel actually means for us, and to live in the benefits it provides. It's hard to accept and live like we have a different relationship with God, different standing with the enemy, and a different life. But we do.

What things that Jesus gave you or did for you do you have trouble believing? Identify those areas, and ask Him to strengthen your belief. Then, as you understand what Christ did for you, look for ways to confirm these truths in others. Build up those in the body of Christ by encouraging them to know and believe what Jesus did for them and who they are in Christ.

Lord, like the father said to Jesus, I say, "I believe. Help my unbelief." You have given me so many gifts through Your Son, but I don't always act like I have those gifts. Help my faith grow stronger so I can walk fully in all that You have already done for me and so I can encourage others. Amen.

NOTES

DAY FIVE
The Blessing of Perspective

"The eye is the lamp of the body. If your eyes are healthy, your whole body will be full of light. But if your eyes are unhealthy, your whole body will be full of darkness. If then the light within you is darkness, how great is that darkness!" Matthew 6:22-23

We all have filters through which we see life, and those filters come from anything and everything: our gender, our race, our life experiences, our birth order, our family of origin, our personality, and much more. All of the characteristics and history of you and your life weave together in a unique way to form a filter through which you view the world. Sometimes the filter lets you see things fairly accurately, and sometimes it distorts them.

This is why reading the Bible is so important. It will fix your faulty filters and give you the right perspective. When you believe that God is who He says He is, He will do what He promised, and you are who He says you are, all of life looks different.

You begin to see things in light of eternity. Temporary things of this world become less important than the purposes and plans of the Sovereign God, who exists outside of time and space. You realize His ways are above our ways, His timing is perfect, and even the bad that happened to you has threads of good. Let the Word of God fix your filters and help your perspective to change.

Lord, give me a desire and hunger for Your Word, and help me to make reading it a priority. Use it to wash my eyes and fix any ways I look at the world or my circumstances that isn't in line with Your Word. In Jesus' name, amen.

NOTES

DAY SIX
The Blessing of Thanksgiving

"Give thanks in all circumstances; for this is God's will for you in Christ Jesus." 1 Thessalonians 5:18

One of the best ways to change your perspective is to practice thankfulness. Ann Voskamp writes,

> How my eyes see, perspective, is my key to enter into His gates. I can only do so with thanksgiving. If my inner eye has God seeping up through all things, then can't I give thanks for anything? And if I can give thanks for the good things, the hard things, the absolute everything, I can enter the gates to glory. Living in His presence is fullness of joy- and seeing shows the way in.

Before you can accept His blessings and allow them to flow through you, you have to recognize their presence in your life. Thanksgiving is the way to do that. Consistently giving Him thanks for small things, big things, wonderful things, and hard things will help you see His hand in your life in ways you did not notice before. You will also begin to see how consistent His actions are with His Word.

The blessings of thanksgiving is summed up best by Hannah Whitall Smith: "This way of seeing our Father in everything makes life one long thanksgiving and gives a rest of heart, and, more than that, a gaiety of spirit, that is unspeakable."

Lord, thank You. For all the good, all the bad, all the ease in life and all the trials, for everything, thank You. As I go through each day, help me see things to thank You for, so I can see You more clearly in my life. I want to enter into Your gates today and every day! Amen!

NOTES

DAY SEVEN
The Blessing of the Upside Down Kingdom

"But many who are first will be last, and the last first."
Mark 10:31

Just as the prophets had predicted, the Messiah, Jesus, established His kingdom. But it was an upside down kingdom. In this realm, the King is a servant (Romans 15:8), those who want to be the King's right-hand man must be a slave to all (Mark 10:43-44), you must give away your life in order to keep it (Luke 17:33), and you are to forgive your enemies, not attack them (Matthew 5:44). In other words, it is nothing like a real kingdom and not at *all* what anyone was expecting.

Jesus explained this upside down kingdom best in a portion of the Sermon on the Mount called the Beatitudes. In it, Jesus said upside down things like those who mourn, those who are meek, those who are poor in spirit, all of them are blessed. Not your typical candidates for blessings.

In our country we have to be law-abiding citizens to stay out of jail, but in this Kingdom His greatest blessings are only available to those who are the lawbreakers and who are imperfect because perfect people don't need grace and mercy. His blessings flow to us no matter who we are or what we've done. Aren't you grateful for an upside down kingdom?

Lord, thank You that when I became saved, I transferred into Your Kingdom (Colossians 1:13), where the blessed life is available to everyone. I open my hands and my heart to receive Your very best blessings today, not because I deserve them, but precisely because I do not -- that's the way Your upside down kingdom works. Thank You, Lord! Amen!

NOTES

DAY EIGHT
The Blessing of a Poor Spirit

"Blessed are the poor in spirit, for theirs is the kingdom of heaven." Matthew 5:3

The first Beatitude listed in Matthew 5 deals with the poor in spirit. In keeping with His upside down kingdom, He says those who are poor in spirit will have the kingdom of heaven. This isn't what the Jews thought at the time, and, if we're honest, it's not what we think, either. We think of heaven as a reward for those who are the best people, for Christians who are strong spiritually, for those who don't mess up.

But even the strongest Christian in your church and even the best person on earth is poor in spirit. All of us, apart from God, are sinful and need Him. The blessings, though, come to those who realize and admit their spiritual destitution.

Everyone is poor in Spirit, but for those who admit it and become spiritual beggars, He flings open the doors of His kingdom and offers it *all* to them. Beggars can't be choosers, but in His upside down kingdom, we don't have to choose because we're given it all.

Lord, I admit the poverty of my own spirit before You. Apart from You, I am nothing but a sinful mess with a powerless, poor spirit. Thank You, Lord, for being the kind of King who gives the most destitute in His spiritual kingdom the entire kingdom. I accept all that You want to give me, not because I deserve it (because I don't) but because You want me to have it. This beggar will not refuse Your offering. In Jesus' name, amen!

NOTES

DAY NINE
The Blessing of Understanding

"What we have received is not the spirit of the world, but the Spirit who is from God, so that we may understand what God has freely given us." 1 Corinthians 2:12

Paul, in the scripture above, seemed to know that the upside down kingdom would be hard to understand. Unconditional love, undeserved grace, unmerited favor, a kingdom given to a beggar -- none of it makes much sense in our world.

But while our own spirit is poor, we have a helper, the "Spirit who is from God," to help us understand our free gifts. With the Holy Spirit to guide us into all truth (John 16:3), we can begin to comprehend the real meaning to our lives of the sacrifice of Jesus on the cross, His defeat of death, and the way His righteousness is imputed, or given, to us. We begin to understand how someone poor in spirit can inherit a kingdom.

Without the Spirit to guide us, we will stay where we are, with free gifts all around us, but unable to understand what they are or what they can do for us. But with the Spirit, the truth becomes more and more plain. 1 Corinthians 2:11 says the Spirit of God is the only one who knows the mind of God. What better guide could we have to lead us into truth?

Holy Spirit, I ask that You would guide me into all truth about each of the gifts You have freely given me. Help me to understand, deep in my soul, everything You have done for me. Teach me what I need to know about each of the things You have done for me and given me, so I can flow in Your blessings. In Jesus' name, amen.

NOTES

DAY TEN
The Blessing of Help

"Guard the good deposit that was entrusted to you—guard it with the help of the Holy Spirit who lives in us."
2 Timothy 1:14

Although we are poor in spirit, God gave us His Spirit, which is rich with blessings. Not only does the Spirit lead us into understanding and truth, but the Spirit also *helps* us.

Paul told Timothy to guard the "good deposit", or truth, that had been given to him with the help of the Holy Spirit. Even after you have been led into "all truth" by the Spirit, if you don't guard it by staying filled with the Holy Spirit and listening to the Spirit when it tries to help you be a good guard, it is possible to lose that truth.

Be sensitive to the Spirit's nudges about what and who to stay away from, what not to watch, and what not to listen to. That is the Spirit helping you be a good guard of the truth. The Spirit will convict you to push you toward the Lord, and toward being more like Him, which will help you guard the truth that is within you.

Listen to what the Spirit is telling *you*, and you'll find it the blessing of help to guard the truth.

Lord, I have not always listened to the urging of Your Spirit when You tell me to stay away from certain people or things, but I want to start fresh. Speak to me in the way only You can, and I will listen. Starting today, I will use the help You give to be a good guard of the truth that You have led me to. In Jesus' name, amen.

NOTES

DAY ELEVEN
The Blessing of Being Equipped

"For the Spirit God gave us does not make us timid, but gives us power, love and self-discipline." 2 Timothy 1:7

Another blessing of the Holy Spirit is that it equips us to live an empowered life as a free child of God who can overcome the flesh to do what He calls us to do.

After the Holy Spirit fell in the upper room on the Day of Pentecost, the Spirit-filled disciples were empowered to do exactly as Jesus had told them to do when He gave them the Great Commission.

Paul, the great apostle, told the Corinthians that he had been with them "in weakness and in fear and in much trembling, and my message and my preaching were not in persuasive words of wisdom." Does that sound like you sometimes when you do what the Lord has asked you to do?

He continued to say, though, that he spoke to them "in demonstration of the Spirit and of power, so that your faith would not rest on the wisdom of men, but on the power of God."

Paul had it right - he did what he did not so that he shined, but so that God did. The Lord used a talking donkey to be a messenger, so He doesn't require much to work with. All He requires is a willing instrument, and He will play all the notes through you. Through His Holy Spirit, He equips those He calls.

Lord, thank You for Your Spirit living in me, to give me power to rise above my own abilities, and to be equipped to do amazing things in my walk with You, so that You can demonstrate Your power through me! Amen!

NOTES

DAY TWELVE
The Blessing of Gifts

"Each of you should use whatever gift you have received to serve others, as faithful stewards of God's grace in its various forms." 1 Peter 4:10

When you are Spirit-filled the Spirit gives you specific spiritual gifts. The gifts of the Spirit are listed and discussed at length four times in the New Testament (in 1 Corinthians 12-14; Romans 12; Ephesians 4; and 1 Peter 4). And, in every single one of these passages, *unity* is also discussed.

While each of us may have different gifts, the purpose of the gifts is to be used as part of a single body. 1 Corinthians 12:27 says, "Now you are the body of Christ, and each one of you is a part of it." We each have a part to play to make the body successful.

Everyone cannot do every job in the church, but everyone is supposed to do something. And not only are they supposed to do something, but they are supposed to do it in conjunction with the others in the body. Your hand doesn't go off by itself into the kitchen to cook dinner (as handy as that would be). The rest of the body goes, too, and all of the pieces of the body work together.

There is no greater or deeper personal fulfillment than operating in the gifts the Spirit has given you. It's another example of His favor flowing to us, by giving us fulfillment in operating in our gifts, and that favor flowing out of us, by using our gifts to serve others for Him.

Lord, help me to recognize, develop and exercise my spiritual gifts. I want to be used by You to build unity and I submit everything I am to You. In Jesus' name, amen.

NOTES

DAY THIRTEEN
The Blessing of the Fruit of the Spirit

"But the fruit of the Spirit is love, joy, peace, forbearance, kindness, goodness, faithfulness, gentleness and self-control." Galatians 5:22-23b

When we're Spirit-filled, our lives bear what Paul calls "fruit." The fruits of the Spirit are for the benefit of those around us, but also for ourselves. A life lived with peace and love and gentleness and all the other fruits is simply a better life, partly because it helps us in our relationships with others.

Doing your part in the body of Christ means you have to work with other people in the same body. Sometimes, you feel a little like chopping off a body part or two because let's all admit it, people are not always fun to deal with and relationships aren't always easy.

Someone once said, "Where there is unity, there are heroes." It takes heroic acts of selflessness to achieve and maintain unity. Fortunately, we don't have to be a hero of our own power. The Spirit empowers us with fruits of love, joy, peace, patience, kindness, goodness, faithfulness, gentleness, and self-control. All of those are required when being a part of any successful group or relationship.

The best way to exhibit this fruit in your life is not to try harder. The key is to stay filled with the Spirit and submit to its help as you become more like Jesus. He will mold and shape you so that everyone sees the fruits of His Spirit at work in and through you.

Lord, my own poor spirit doesn't have the same fruit as Your Spirit. Do Your work in me so when people see me, they see the fruit of the Holy Spirit. In Jesus' name, amen!

NOTES

DAY FOURTEEN
The Blessing of Mourning

"Blessed are those who mourn, for they will be comforted." Matthew 5:4

Mourning. It's not a word that needs defining. But of the several Greek words related to sadness, the one used in Matthew 5:4 is the one on the farthest end of the spectrum, the heaviest. It's the sadness felt when someone dies and it denotes not just tears, but sobbing.

Each of us has mourned. We've had loss that changed the shape of our world, creating space where there once was no space. Shattered dreams changed our plans. Broken hearts changed our path in life. We have mourned because of changes we didn't want, changes we couldn't control, changes we can't change back.

But what happens after the mourning begins depends on your relationship with the Lord.

When a child of God mourns, she doesn't mourn like those who have no hope. No, a child of God knows that she has the hope that good can and will come from every situation (Romans 8:28), that there is Someone to call out to for peace that passes understanding (Phil 4:7), that she knows the One who came to bind up the broken heart (Isaiah 61:1; Psalm 147:3), that He will save those crushed in spirit (Psalm 34:18), and He can turn mourning into dancing (Psalm 30:11). And, yes, that there will be comfort, just as Jesus said.

Lord, thank You for Your promises to bind up my broken heart, to give me peace that passes understanding, and that good will come from my loss. Thank You that when I mourn, I will be comforted. In Jesus' name, amen.

NOTES

Romans 8:28 And we know that in (all) things God works for the good of those who love Him.

Phil 4:7 And the peace of God which trancends all understanding will guard your hearts and your minds in Christ Jesus.

Isiah 61:1 He came to bind up the broken hearted Psalm 147:3

DAY FIFTEEN
The Blessing of Comfort

"Why, my soul, are you downcast? Why so disturbed within me? Put your hope in God, for I will yet praise him, my Savior and my God." Psalm 42:5-6a

Comfort. That's what He promises us when we mourn. Not to inherit the earth, or inherit His kingdom -- because He knew that no amount of promises of inheritance or gifts would make us feel better when we're sad.

According to the Psalmist, He creates this beautiful exchange, removing, actually taking away, our mourning clothes, and replacing those mourning clothes with gladness, and replacing our mourning with dancing (Psalm 30:11). He exchanges our ashes for beauty, our mourning for the oil of gladness, and our spirit of despair for a garment of praise (Isaiah 61:3).

And why? "[T]o the end that my glory may sing praise to You and not be silent. O Lord my God, I will give thanks to You forever" (Psalm 30:12). "They will be called oaks of righteousness, a planting of the LORD for the display of his splendor" (Isaiah 61:4).

After His exchange, we have glory, and are oaks of righteousness, so that we may sing praise and give thanks to Him forever, and be the display of His splendor.

Lord, when hard times come and change happens that I don't want, I will claim Your promises of comfort and the beautiful exchange You provide for me. Make me an oak of righteousness, for the display of Your splendor. In Jesus' name, amen.

NOTES

DAY SIXTEEN
The Blessing of Meekness

"Blessed are the meek, for they will inherit the earth."
Matthew 5:5

Before Jesus used the word, the Greeks used "meekness" mainly to describe inanimate things, like light, wind, and sound, that have a spectrum of power, and "meek" meant they had the ability to be much stronger or more powerful than what they were currently exhibiting.

Then, Jesus came along and said, "I am meek." To (heavily) paraphrase, he was saying, "I have a great deal more power than I am exhibiting to you. I'm holding back. I'm being reserved. Because it is not my purpose to show you all of my power. It is my purpose to obey my Father and do His will."

We women have a lot of power in our relationships. Sometimes, we wield that power in ways that may get us what we want, but in the process we create damage and end up hurting ourselves or others.

The idea of being meek is scary. We worry that if we don't use the power we have, we will never get what we want or need. And yet Jesus said, if you're meek, you inherit the earth. So, you'll not just get what you need or want, you'll get it all. Controlling others, or manipulating them to get what we want, isn't His plan for us. His desire is to be the source of all of our needs. It's another example of His upside down kingdom: when you *don't* show power, you get everything.

Lord, make me more like You so I am meek in my relationships. I trust You to give me all I need physically, emotionally, and spiritually. In Jesus' name, Amen.

NOTES

DAY SEVENTEEN
The Blessing of a Quiet Answer

"A quiet answer turns away wrath." Proverbs 18:21

One Bible commentator said meekness is "patience in the reception of injuries." Drive in any urban city or read comments online or even spend a little time in your own home and you can see that finding someone who is patient in the reception of injuries is hard to come by.

The Greeks used the word "meek" sometimes to refer to horses that had been put under submission by having a bit placed in their mouth. It's so symbolic that this form of meekness came because of an animal's mouth being controlled. James said, "When we put bits into the mouths of horses to make them obey us, we can turn the whole animal" (James 3:3). He then went on to talk about the tongue, saying that it's a small part of the body, but it can set the course for an entire life. Solomon put it this way, "Life and death is in the tongue."

David knew how hard it was to control his words. So he prayed, "Set a guard over my mouth, LORD; keep watch over the door of my lips". He was giving the reins of the bit in his mouth to God.

1 Peter 3:9 says, "Do not repay evil with evil or insult with insult. On the contrary, repay evil with blessing, because to this you were called so that you may inherit a blessing." Inheriting a blessing, repaying evil with a blessing... there's the flow. Words of blessing out, blessing in, all because of meekness.

Lord, help me to control my tongue because I want to speak life. I want to respond to insults with blessings. I want to give quiet answers. In Jesus' name, amen.

NOTES

DAY EIGHTEEN
The Blessing of Unfading Beauty

"Your beauty should not come from outward adornment, such as elaborate hairstyles and the wearing of gold jewelry or fine clothes. Rather, it should be that of your inner self, the unfading beauty of a gentle and quiet spirit, which is of great worth in God's sight." 1 Peter 3:3-4

Meekness, at its core, means holding back so that something greater can be accomplished in your life and the lives of those around you. It means laying aside pride and reining in your flesh, giving everything over to the Lord and letting Him do all the work to get you where He wants you to be, and letting Him supply all of your needs according to His riches in glory.

When you are humble and let Him be in charge, He can and will pour blessings into your life.

His Word is filled with promises for the meek, blessings just for the humble. He promises peace, prosperity, favor, and an inheritance. He promises to make sure the meek are honored, exalted and lifted up in due time. He promises to sustain them, to give them victory, and to guide them and teach them.

Meekness is the kind of beauty that doesn't fade, and is of such great worth to the Lord that He pours out blessings to you, which you can then use to bless others.

Lord, I want there to be less of me and more of You. Let Your work in me produce a gentle and humble attitude, so that meekness is a hallmark of my life, and so that Your blessings can flow in and through me in a greater way than ever before. In Jesus' name, amen!

NOTES

DAY NINETEEN
The Blessing of Hunger and Thirst for Righteousness

"Blessed are those who hunger and thirst for righteousness, for they will be filled." Matthew 5:6

Hunger and thirst are signals that we need to fill a void, fill our emptiness, so that life can continue. If we ignore those signals, eventually we'll die; if we respond, we'll live.

Jesus knew there was a void we *all* have, caused by the separation from God as a result of the fall of mankind in the Garden of Eden. He knew that each of us hunger and thirst, not just in the physical sense, but emotionally and spiritually.

It may be a tired cliché, but it's true: there is a God-shaped hole in all of us that only He can fill. When we listen to the signals of hunger and thirst for Him and allow Him to fill the emptiness, to be the Bread of Life and the Living Water that never runs dry, we are blessed with a sense of being filled and fulfilled.

From that place of spiritual health, not only are you blessed, but so is everyone around you. Living a life filled with Him will nourish your family, your friends, your coworkers, and everyone else because you will be interacting with them not from a position of neediness or emptiness, but from fulfillment and wholeness in Him.

Lord, thank You for filling me when I'm hungry and thirsty for You, my righteousness. Thank You for the blessing of a life of fulfillment in You, that blesses me and everyone around me, as Your Living Water overflows and Bread of Life multiplies through me. I hunger and thirst for more of You, and less of me. In Jesus' name, amen.

NOTES

DAY TWENTY
The Blessing of the True God

"Do people make their own gods? Yes, but they are not gods!" Jeremiah 16:20

In Bible times, people turned to something else instead of God to meet their needs. This was called idolatry. We tend to stand back on this side of human progress and think, how could they have been so dumb?

But they simply did in the physical realm what we now do in our innermost being. They literally set up something else as the one to meet their needs and they called it what it was -- a god. Now, we do the same thing, turning to substitutes that cheer us up, chill us out, excite us, or help us escape... we just don't call it a god. But an actual statue of a god is not required for idolatry. Idolatry is nothing more than trying to use a substitute for what only God can do.

Jesus once told a woman at a well that whoever drank of the water of that well would get thirsty again. It's the same for our substitutes. We use them to fill the void for a while, but we get thirsty again. But Jesus said, "Whoever drinks the water I give them will never thirst. Indeed, the water I give them will become in them a spring of water welling up to eternal life" (John 4:14).

Only one thing truly satisfies, and that is Jesus, the spring of living water. He is our righteousness, the righteousness after which we should hunger and thirst. He is the one – the only one -- that fills the void within us.

Lord, show me if I have any substitutes in my life that I use to try to fill a void that only You can fill. Help me to shift my appetite so that it craves You more than anything else. In Jesus' name, amen!

NOTES

DAY TWENTY-ONE
The Blessing of Seeking

"You will seek me and find me when you seek me with all your heart." Jeremiah 29:13

We all feel the hunger and the thirst inside — that part is easy. But directing that need toward Jesus, our righteousness, requires action on our part. It sometimes requires changing our appetite.

When we are hungry in our bodies, we generally go and actively seek out food. When we are thirsty, we get a drink. We take action to get what we need, and we make that action a priority.

It is the same with our spiritual lives. We can't be filled by Him if we don't seek him. We have to make it a priority to seek Him. We have to set up a constant and consistent intake of nourishment for our soul. He is the spring of Living Water, but if we don't drink from the spring, it does us no good. He's the Bread of Life, but if we don't eat, then how does it help us?

Isaiah 55:1, 11 says, "Come, all you who are thirsty, come to the waters; and you who have no money, come, buy and eat!.... The LORD will guide you always; he will satisfy your needs in a sun-scorched land and will strengthen your frame. You will be like a well-watered garden, like a spring whose waters never fail."

Lord, I seek after You today. I feel like I'm in a sun-scorched land and I need You to guide me and strengthen me, to make me like a well-watered garden. Fill me to overflowing so I can bless others, too. Open my heart and teach me what it means to hunger after You and You alone. In Jesus' name, amen.

NOTES

DAY TWENTY-TWO
The Blessing of Being Merciful

"Blessed are the merciful, for they will be shown mercy." Matthew 5:7

Mercy reaches down into suffering and does what it can to ease the pain.

The principle in Matthew 5:7 is a universal truth: the more you give and help others in their time of suffering and need, the more you will receive in turn. If you keep your fists clenched tight when it's time to give, those same closed fists will keep you from receiving. But if you give freely, you will receive freely.

It's all about the flow.

But we aren't just middlemen, so that the flow only goes from God, to us, to others, and then stops. In actuality, the flow keeps going, and comes back to us in the form of various blessings.

It's like a two-way street. God fills us with His love, we then show that love by being merciful to others, and then we receive mercy, too. We receive twice, while we only give out once. With God, it's always like that because you can never out-give Him; He will always give more than you or I can ever give.

Lord, show me what it means to be merciful. I want to be more like You, and over and over You have shown Your mercy, even to those who did not deserve it (like me). Give me opportunities to do the same, and to be merciful, so that I may obtain mercy. In Jesus' name, amen.

NOTES

DAY TWENTY-THREE
The Blessing of Being Enough

"At the present time your plenty will supply what they need...." 2 Corinthians 8:14a

We are called to help each other, and instructed to do so. But it isn't always easy, is it?

We don't know what to do to help, we don't want to offend or overstep, we don't want to be a bother, we feel self-conscious, we assume someone else is going to do it, and we feel like whatever we can say or do isn't enough.

It's much easier to be the priest and the Levite in the story of the Good Samaritan, and to walk on by the man in misery. But Jesus told that story to show what we're supposed to do – stop and help our fellow man. And the Samaritan didn't nurse the beaten man back to health, or do all the work – in fact, he just took him to a hotel, helped him get through one night, then paid someone else to tend to the man and left him there.

Sometimes we may think that helping others requires more than it actually does. God will only call you to do what He knows you can do. The Samaritan spent much more money than he did time helping the beaten man, probably because that's the way he could help the best.

God used what the Samaritan had, and He will use what we have, as long as we, like the Samaritan, are willing to be of help. All He asks of you is to use what He's given you.

Lord, thank You that You do not ask more of us than we can handle. Open my eyes to see those around me and the simple ways I can help, using what I have. In Jesus' name, amen.

NOTES

DAY TWENTY-FOUR
The Blessing of Your Suffering

"Because [Jesus] himself suffered when he was tempted, he is able to help those who are being tempted." Hebrews 2:18

God helps people through people, *always*. One of the jobs we have as the body of Christ is to be the physical manifestation of Christ; we are the ones who must act as His hands and feet to those who are in need of relief from suffering.

All of us have different gifts, and different ways we are called to help others in their suffering. Your gifts and life experiences have uniquely positioned you to be Christ's hands and feet to certain people who are suffering.

Your suffering taught you how others who go through something similar will need help. Your blessings are distinctively shaped to help meet someone's need. Your knowledge is perfectly suited to lessen another's burdens.

Even your temptations and sins with which you struggle can help others, if you are willing to share your experiences. Too often, though, we hide what we fight against. But if Jesus had never told someone else what happened in the wilderness when Satan came to tempt him, we wouldn't have a blueprint for how to use the Word to fight the enemy.

Our suffering and our struggles can and will help others, if we open up and let ourselves be used.

Lord, help me to have the faith in You that I need to step out and be the one through whom You alleviate the misery of others. I want to flow in Your blessings. In Jesus' name, amen!

NOTES

DAY TWENTY-FIVE
The Blessing of Purity of Heart

"Blessed are the pure in heart, for they shall see God." Matthew 5:8

Jesus often spoke against the Pharisees, a sect of Jews who were fanatics about following the law of Moses, and particularly its rules regarding purity and outward appearance. Jesus said about them, "Everything they do is done for people to see" (Matthew 23:5).

So, put in historical context, it is no surprise that Jesus would say, "Blessed are the pure in *heart.*" Jesus was (and is!) always more concerned about what was happening on the inside of a person. He would heal people of their outward infirmities, but He would also forgive them of their inward sins.

But our inside can only be pure through the blood and sacrifice of Jesus, and by accepting His position as Lord of our lives so that we submit to what He wants to do in us. Then, He will work on us to move the reality of our hearts closer and closer to the purity of the blood that covers us.

During this process, we will see God, as Jesus promised, not just in the afterlife, but here, today, working in us and around us to make us into who He wants us to be. In turn, those around us will begin to see what flows from a heart that is given over to the cleansing, sanctifying work of Christ. It's yet another blessing that flows.

Lord, I surrender my heart to You and submit to Your plans for the remodel of my heart. Make me more like You. Cleanse me, purify me, and sanctify me, to bring me closer to the purity of Your blood. In Jesus' name, amen.

NOTES

DAY TWENTY-SIX
The Blessing of the Greatest Commandments

Jesus replied: "Love the Lord your God with all your heart and with all your soul and with all your mind.' This is the first and greatest commandment. And the second is like it: 'Love your neighbor as yourself.' All the Law and the Prophets hang on these two commandments."
Matthew 22:37-40

When your attention is constantly and consistently directed toward loving Him with all of your heart, soul, mind, and strength, you begin to see Him and see His hand in everything. His love for you becomes more and more evident, whether it is the joy that comes from a beautiful sunset, or the peace that comes from His presence in times of trouble. It is the deepening of a relationship.

The love of others is the second commandment because you can't love others until you love God and understand His unconditional love for you. The love of others flows from Him, and sometimes the love we show isn't our own, but His through us. When you focus on loving others, who are His creation that He loves just as much as He loves you, and take the opportunity to be His hands and feet to them, you are given a front row seat to watching Him act out His love for others. You are the conduit for the love He wants to pour out on others, and watching it happen is a special blessing all on its own.

Lord, help me love You today and show me ways I can love You more. And help me love others, and see them the way You see them. I can't wait to see the favor flowing to and through me as I begin to love You and love others more! In Jesus' name, amen!

NOTES

DAY TWENTY-SEVEN
The Blessing of Making Peace

"Blessed are the peacemakers, for they will be called children of God." Matthew 5:9

As women, we set the emotional tone in our home and our relationships, so when we are at peace, we become makers of peace. But the world around us is not very conducive to peaceful living. People irritate us, hard things happen to us, unknown futures await us – how can we be peaceful?

Philippians 4:6-7 says that peace will come when we, in everything, let our requests be made known to God in prayer and supplication, with thanksgiving. That's a complex sentence, so let's unpack it a bit.

The first part means we don't just take the things that have gotten horribly bad to God, but *every*thing, so we'll be talking to Him a lot, and often.

And then we're to add the component of thankfulness about it all. When we do, we will cultivate a sense of gratefulness and a realization of His many blessings toward us. This, in turn, builds our faith as we see all that He does for us, even in the face of difficulty.

Then, the Bible says, "And the peace of God, which surpasses all comprehension, will guard your hearts and your minds in Christ Jesus." So, more peace than we can even comprehend will be ours, and it will guard our hearts and our minds, the two sources of un-peaceful emotions.

Lord, today I claim the peace that surpasses all comprehension, and I claim it as a guard over my heart and mind in Jesus Christ. Thank You for Your peace! Amen!

NOTES

DAY TWENTY-EIGHT
The Blessing of Choosing Peace

"[A] future awaits those who seek peace." Psalms 37:37b

Peace is a fruit of the Spirit, but you have to choose to give the Spirit the control before your life bears that fruit.

Part of making the choice for peace is to follow the leading of the Spirit away from the things that are triggers or pitfalls for you to lose His peace. You can't find peace in doing the same old things that you've always done that have led to your life being filled with drama, worry, and fear.

When you choose to be Spirit-filled, Spirit-led, and Spirit-controlled, then you are able to be peace-filled.

And when we choose peace, we naturally become peacemakers. We make peace occur around us because we are filled with peace, and we really can't help but create peace wherever we go.

James said that peacemakers who sow in peace reap a harvest of righteousness (James 3:18). The idea of sowing peace, like seeds, is a beautiful representation of what happens. When seeds are sown, they are scattered and thrown around the farmer as he goes along the rows. Wherever he goes, he leaves seeds. Then, later, a harvest comes. This passage tells us that from peace seeds come righteousness. That is the legacy we will leave as peacemakers.

Lord, I want to live in Your peace, and have so much of it that it overflows wherever I go. I want to sow peace so that I reap a harvest of righteousness in my home, my job, and my relationships. Thank You for making peace a possibility in this crazy world. In Jesus' name, amen!

NOTES

DAY TWENTY-NINE
The Blessing of Persecution

"Blessed are those who are persecuted because of righteousness, for theirs is the kingdom of heaven." Matthew 5:10

We are called to be the light of the world and to shine His light into the darkness. The darkness, though, doesn't always happily receive the light. When a bright light is shined into your eyes first thing in the morning, it's so shocking and painful that you hide your eyes from it. You don't welcome it. You reject it, sometimes quite loudly!

Other times, you are in the dark and looking for something, and someone shines a light. This time you're much more likely to say, "Thank you, that's what I needed!"

It is the same for those living in spiritual darkness. Light represents something completely different and opposite from what they are used to. Sometimes the light is welcomed because they are searching for something more, and sometimes it is flatly rejected, possibly in ways that aren't kind.

It might be that your light is one of the first shone and it is too hard for the person to accept this time, but the longer the light shines, the more used to it she will get, and eventually she will come to accept the light as better than the darkness. It's your job to shine, and you'll be blessed no matter the reaction or the outcome.

Lord, guide me as I shine Your light into darkness. Give me wisdom on when to be open, based not on my own judgments of how a person will receive it, but in obedience to Your urging, so I can successfully share the gospel and lead others to You. In Jesus' name, amen!

NOTES

DAY THIRTY
Blessing of Suffering for the Gospel

"Blessed are you when men hate you, when they exclude you and insult you and reject your name as evil, because of the Son of Man." Luke 6:22

More than any other path to blessing, persecution might be the hardest for us. The thing is, if we are going to be His disciples, then we *will* be persecuted. It automatically comes with the territory.

The key to flowing in blessing even while being persecuted or rejected about your faith is this: "Do not repay evil with evil or insult with insult, but with blessing, because to this you were called *so that you may inherit a blessing*" (1 Peter 3:9).

Jesus said, "Love your enemies, do good to them, and lend to them without expecting to get anything back. Then *your reward will be great*, and you will be sons of the Most High, because he is kind to the ungrateful and wicked" (Luke 6:35).

Not only will you be blessed in general, but when you are persecuted, *"the Spirit of glory and of God rests on you"* (1 Peter 4:14).

Although we're guaranteed to suffer persecution, we're also guaranteed blessings when it happens. Those blessings will, in turn, strengthen us to spread the news about Him, which will result in people coming to Him.

Lord, give me an opportunity to share Your Word with someone. Help me to have the courage and give me the right words, but if it is not accepted, thank You that You will bless me in ways that only You can. In Jesus' name, amen!

NOTES

DAY THIRTY-ONE
The Blessing of Blessings

"But since you excel in everything--in faith, in speech, in knowledge, in complete earnestness and in the love we have kindled in you --see that you also excel in this grace of giving." 2 Corinthians 8:7

God's blessings are amazing because, like their Maker, they do not follow the laws of nature.

Nature says perpetual motion is not possible, but His blessings have the power of perpetual motion and can continue moving indefinitely. He does not intend for His blessings to you to stop with you. He gives to you so that you can then give to others, and so the blessings keep moving from person to person to person.

Nature says matter cannot be created, but like the two loaves and five fishes that fed 5,000, small blessings can create bigger ones. You may feel like you don't have much to give to others, but if you give from what you've been given, He takes it and multiplies it in ways we could never predict.

Nature says that the only way to keep something is to not transfer it away. But the best way to stay blessed is to give blessings away. You cannot receive unless you are a giver, and you cannot outgive God.

Be the conduit of His blessings today, and let them flow from you to others, and be amazed at what our God can do through you!

Lord, I thank You for each of the innumerable blessings You have given me. Take each blessing, and use me to let it flow to others, to be a blessing that keeps going, keeps giving, and keeps growing. In Jesus' name, amen!

NOTES